DAVY CROCKETT

Andrea P. Smith

Published in 2012 by The Rosen Publishing Group, Inc.
29 East 21st Street, New York, NY 10010

First Edition

Editor: Joanne Randolph
Book Design: Planman Technologies
Illustrations: Planman Technologies

Library of Congress Cataloging-in-Publication Data

Smith, Andrea P.
Davy Crockett / by Andrea P. Smith. — 1st ed.
    p. cm. — (Jr. graphic American legends)
Includes index.
ISBN 978-1-4488-5192-8 (library binding) — ISBN 978-1-4488-5222-2 (pbk.) — ISBN 978-1-4488-5223-9 (6-pack)
1. Crockett, Davy, 1786–1836—Juvenile literature. 2. Pioneers—Tennessee—Biography—Juvenile literature. 3. Frontier and pioneer life—Tennessee—Juvenile literature. 4. Tennessee—Biography—Juvenile literature. 5. Legislators—United States—Biography—Juvenile literature. 6. United States. Congress. House—Biography—Juvenile literature. 7. Alamo (San Antonio, Tex.)—Siege, 1836—Juvenile literature. 8. Crockett, Davy, 1786–1836—Comic books, strips, etc. 9. Pioneers—Tennessee—Biography—Comic books, strips, etc. 10. Alamo (San Antonio, Tex.)—Siege, 1836—Comic books, strips, etc. 11. Graphic novels. I. Title.
F436.C95S63 2012
976.8'04092—dc22
[B]

2011001718

Manufactured in the United States of America

CPSIA Compliance Information: Batch #PLS1102PK: For Further Information contact Rosen Publishing, New York, New York at 1-800-237-9932

Contents

Main Characters

Davy Crockett (1786–1836) A **frontiersman** and **politician**. He became a **legend** and a folk hero. He died at the Alamo.

William B. Travis (1809–1836) Scout in the Texas army. He **commanded** the forces in the Battle of the Alamo.

Antonio López de Santa Anna (1794–1876) Army officer and president of Mexico. He led the assault on the Alamo and had all the Texas defenders killed.

Elizabeth Patton Crockett (1788–1860) Married Davy Crockett in 1815. Elizabeth was born in North Carolina and died in Acton, Texas. A monument in her honor as a pioneer woman stands in Acton.

DAVY CROCKETT

LEGEND SAYS THAT WHEN DAVY CROCKETT WAS A BOY IN TENNESSEE, HE KILLED A BEAR. HE WAS JUST THREE YEARS OLD.

YEE HAW!

ONE DAY, THEY SAY, HE SWALLOWED A LIGHTNING BOLT.

GIDDY UP!

ANOTHER DAY, HE RODE AN ALLIGATOR UP NIAGARA FALLS.

EVERYONE LIKED TO TELL STORIES ABOUT DAVY, INCLUDING DAVY!

DID I EVER TELL YOU ABOUT THE TIME I WAS ALMOST EATEN BY A GIANT SNAKE?

YOU HAVE THE BEST ADVENTURES.

DAVY EVEN WROTE AN **AUTOBIOGRAPHY** ABOUT HIMSELF.

THEY'LL LOVE THIS STORY.

DAVY CROCKETT WAS A REAL MAN, THOUGH. HE GREW UP ON THE BANKS OF THE LIMESTONE RIVER IN TENNESSEE.

DAVY, YOU'RE OLD ENOUGH FOR YOUR FIRST RIFLE.

THANKS, PA.

DAVY LOVED TO GO INTO THE WILDERNESS AND HUNT.

I'M BACK. LOOK WHAT I BROUGHT HOME.

YOU'VE TURNED INTO A REAL GOOD HUNTER, SON.

WHEN DAVY WAS TWELVE, HIS FATHER SENT HIM ON A **CATTLE DRIVE.**

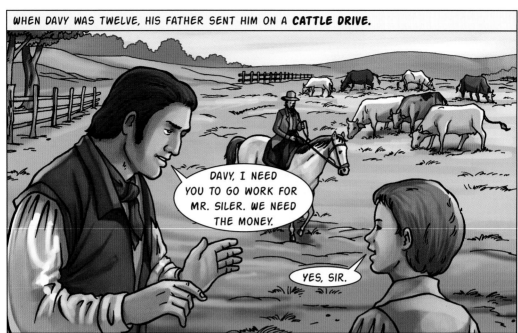

SEVERAL YEARS LATER, DAVY CROCKETT MARRIED MARY FINLEY, WHO WAS CALLED POLLY. THEY STARTED THEIR OWN FAMILY AND MOVED TO AN AREA WHERE MANY CREEK INDIANS LIVED.

CROCKETT ENDED UP SERVING TWO TERMS IN THE MILITIA. WHEN HE RETURNED HOME, HE HAD BEEN **PROMOTED** TO A THIRD SERGEANT.

AFTER POLLY DIED GIVING BIRTH, DAVY CROCKETT MARRIED ELIZABETH PATTON. THE FAMILY THEN MOVED TO WESTERN TENNESSEE.

BE CAREFUL, DAVY.

I'LL BE BACK HOME ONCE I GET A BEAR OR TWO FOR OUR SUPPER.

LISTEN TO THE HOUNDS.

THEY KNOW THERE'S A BEAR NEARBY.

I GOTCHA NOW!

* 600 POUNDS = 272 KG

IN ANOTHER STORY, PEOPLE SAID DAVY COULD GRIN A RACCOON DOWN FROM A TREE.

COME ON DOWN, RACCOON.

HI THERE.

ONCE WHEN DAVY CROCKETT THOUGHT A BRANCH WAS A RACCOON, HE GRINNED ALL THE BARK OFF THE TREE.

IN 1827, CROCKETT WAS ELECTED TO THE **HOUSE OF REPRESENTATIVES.**

DAVY CROCKETT WORKED HARD TO HELP FARMERS AND FRONTIERSMEN.

CROCKETT SERVED TWO TERMS IN CONGRESS. AFTER LOSING HIS THIRD ELECTION, HE WENT BACK HOME TO TENNESSEE.

SANTA ANNA, LEADER OF THE MEXICAN ARMY, AND HIS MEN SURROUNDED THE ALAMO. WILLIAM B. TRAVIS LED THE TEXAN FORCES IN **DEFENSE** AGAINST SANTA ANNA'S 13-DAY SIEGE.

DAVY CROCKETT FOUGHT BRAVELY ALONGSIDE THE OTHER ALAMO DEFENDERS, BUT SANTA ANNA'S ARMY WAS TOO STRONG. ALL THE ALAMO DEFENDERS DIED THAT DAY, INCLUDING CROCKETT.

OVER THE YEARS, DAVY CROCKETT'S FAME GREW.

THIS DAVY CROCKETT SURE WAS BRAVE.

LOOK HOW HE FOUGHT THAT BEAR.

THE *DAVY CROCKETT ALMANACK* WAS PUBLISHED FOR YEARS AFTER HIS DEATH.

I WISH I COULD BE LIKE DAVY CROCKETT.

ME TOO.

IN THE 1950S, THERE WAS A TV SHOW ABOUT DAVY'S LIFE.

IN 1960, THERE WAS A MOVIE ABOUT DAVY CROCKETT CALLED *THE ALAMO*.

JOHN WAYNE IS THE PERFECT DAVY CROCKETT.

HE'S MY FAVORITE ACTOR.

IN LIMESTONE, TENNESSEE, WHERE DAVY WAS BORN, THERE'S ALSO A PARK HONORING THIS AMERICAN LEGEND'S LIFE.

HE WAS A REAL HERO, WASN'T HE?

BOY, DAVY CROCKETT SURE WAS A GREAT MAN.

HE SURE WAS.

Timeline

August 17, 1786 Davy Crockett is born in Limestone, Tennessee.

1798 Twelve-year-old Davy works for Jacob Siler on a cattle drive.

1799 Davy runs away from Siler and returns home.

August 16, 1806 Davy Crockett marries Mary (Polly) Finley.

1811 Davy, Polly, and their two sons move to Lincoln County, Tennessee.

1813 Crockett becomes a scout in the Tennessee militia during the Creek War.

1815 Crockett returns home from the Creek War. Polly dies giving birth to a daughter.

1816 Crockett marries Elizabeth Patton, who has two children of her own.

1822 Crockett moves his family to western Tennessee.

1827 Crockett is elected to the House of Representatives.

1834 Davy Crockett publishes his autobiography, *A Narrative of the Life of David Crockett of the State of Tennessee.*

1836 Crockett moves to Texas and joins the Texas army. He is killed at the Battle of the Alamo on March 6, 1836.

Glossary

Alamo (AL-a-mo) A mission that was turned into a fort. It is located in San Antonio, Texas.

attacked (uh-TAKD) Started a fight with.

autobiography (ah-toh-by-AH-gruh-fee) The story of a person's life written by that person.

cattle drive (KA-tul DRYV) When cattle is moved from one place to another.

commanded (KAH-men-dud) Took charge.

defense (dih-FENTS) Something that saves from harm.

frontiersman (frun-TEERZ-mun) Man who lives and works in an area that has not yet been settled.

House of Representatives (HOWS UV reh-prih-ZEN-tuh-tivs) A part of Congress, which is the law-making body of the U.S. government.

legend (LEH-jend) A person who has been famous and honored for a very long time.

militia (muh-LIH-shuh) A group of people who are trained and ready to fight when needed.

outlandish (OWT-lan-dish) Hard to believe.

politician (pah-lih-TIH-shun) A person who holds or runs for a public office.

promoted (pruh-MOHT-ed) To be raised in rank or importance.

protect (pruh-TEKT) To keep safe.

scout (SKOWT) A person who is sent ahead to explore an area and then report back to a group leader.

swear (SWER) Promise to do something.

tavern (TA-vurn) A place to spend the night and/or eat a meal.

Index

Web Sites

Due to the changing nature of Internet links, Power Kids Press has developed an online list of Web sites related to the subject of this book. This site is updated regularly. Please use this link to access the list:

www.powerkidslinks.com/JGAM/crocket